**GEORGE ORWELL**

# GEORGE ORWELL

Nigel Flynn

# Life and Works

Jane Austen
The Brontës
Thomas Hardy
Hemingway
D.H. Lawrence
Katherine Mansfield
George Orwell
Shakespeare
H.G. Wells
Virginia Woolf

Cover illustration by David Armitage

First published in 1989 by
Wayland (Publishers) Ltd
61 Western Road, Hove
East Sussex BN3 1JD, England

© Copyright 1989 Wayland (Publishers) Ltd

Series adviser: Dr Cornelia Cook
Series designer: David Armitage
Editor: Sophie Davies
Picture research: Liz Miller

**British Library Cataloguing in Publication Data**
Flynn, Nigel
   George Orwell. – (Life and works)
   1. Fiction in English. Orwell, George, 1903–1950
   I. Title   II. Series
   823′.912

ISBN 1-85210-492-9

Typeset by: L. George & R. Gibbs, Wayland
Printed in Italy by G. Canale C.S.p.A., Turin
Bound in the UK by Maclehose & Partners, Portsmouth

# Contents

# 1 The Lost Paradise

'It was a bright cold day in April, and the clocks were striking thirteen'. Thus George Orwell begins *Nineteen Eighty-Four*, the novel that introduced into the English language Newspeak, Big Brother, Doublethink and the Thought Police. Winston Smith, the book's central character, is 39 years old with 'a varicose ulcer above his right ankle'. He works at the Ministry of Truth where he rewrites history and spreads lies. On 4 April 1984 he sits down at a table in his cramped, dingy room in Victory Mansions, London, and begins writing a diary. Not an unusual or an extreme act, one might think. But in the world of *Nineteen Eighty-Four* it is an act of rebellion of such enormity that Winston feels that he is signing his death warrant.

In *Nineteen Eighty-Four* Orwell described what could happen if certain political trends he saw in his own day were fully realized. The novel is set in a totalitarian world in which there is no individual freedom, no privacy, no truth, no love, no decency of any kind; nothing but fear, hatred and pain. Big Brother, the dictator of Oceania, is all-powerful, all-knowing and all-seeing. As Orwell describes it:

*Opposite* On first meeting George Orwell in 1935, a friend described him as 'a tall, big-headed man, with pale-blue, defensively humorous eyes, a little moustache and a painfully snickering laugh'.

> Always the eyes watching you and the voice enveloping you. Asleep or awake, working or eating, indoors or out of doors, in the bath or in bed – no escape. Nothing was your own except the few cubic centimetres inside your skull.

For Orwell writing was a political act, 'using the word "political" ', as he defined it in the essay 'Why I Write' (1947):

> . . . in the widest possible sense. Desire to push the world in a certain direction, to alter people's ideas of the kind of society that they should strive after . . . Every line of serious work that I have written since 1936 has been written, directly or indirectly, against totalitarianism and for democratic socialism, as I understand it. It seems to me nonsense, in a period like our own, to think that one can avoid writing of such subjects. Everyone writes of them in one guise or another. It is simply a question of which side one takes and what approach one follows.

*Orwell's father, Richard Walmesley Blair (second from right, front row). He was 59 when he joined the army in 1916. He was a reserved, aloof man, and saw little of Eric during the formative years of his son's life.*

George Orwell was born Eric Arthur Blair on 25 June 1903 at Motihari in Bengal, India, where his father Richard Walmesley Blair was serving as an official in the Opium Department of the Government of India. Eric was the second of three children. Marjorie, his elder sister, was

*Born in Bengal on 25 June 1903, Eric was six weeks old when this photograph of him, held by an Indian ayah or nanny, was taken. In the following year he was taken by his mother to live in England.*

born in 1898, also in India, and a younger sister, Avril, was born in 1908 after their mother, Ida Blair, had returned with Eric and Marjorie to England. Richard Blair was 46 when Eric was born and barely saw his son until Eric was eight. As was the custom among officials of the Indian Civil Service, Richard Blair remained in India when his wife and children returned to England in 1904.

Ida Blair, twenty years her husband's junior, was from all accounts a quite different person from him. She was artistic, lively and mildly unconventional, supporting the feminist cause and votes for women. On her return to England she settled in Henley-on-Thames, Oxfordshire, living first in a house called 'Ermadale' and then, in 1907, moving to 'The Nutshell', Western Road. Her diary for 1905 records her concern for Eric's health. He already showed signs of a weak chest and suffered from frequent bouts of bronchitis, an affliction he was to bear throughout his life and which finally resulted in tuberculosis, the cause of his death at the age of 46 in 1950. Aptly for the author of *Nineteen Eighty-Four*, his first word was 'beastly'.

Eric's life up to the age of eight seems to have been happy in a conventional way. Born into what he later described as the 'lower-upper-middle-class', he became aware at a very early age of the intricacies of the English class system, or so he was to claim thirty years later in *The Road to Wigan Pier* (1937). His was a 'shabby-genteel family', never having quite enough money to support a style of life to which they considered themselves entitled, but because of their class having to keep up the appearance of doing so. They were, says Orwell, members of the 'landless gentry'. Such social pretensions were common among 'Anglo-Indian' families in England: families like the Blairs who had served in India for one or more generations, in whom notions of 'service' and 'honour' and 'respectability' ran deep, and who had enjoyed privileges that they could ill afford when at the end of their careers abroad, they returned 'home' to England.

**Opposite** *Eric's mother, Ida Blair. She was eighteen years younger than her husband and was, said her son, 'half emancipated, half artistic'.*

**Below** *Indian bearers carrying a party of Englishwomen and their children. British families in India, such as the Blairs, enjoyed privileges and a quality of life few could afford in England.*

From Orwell's own account in 'Why I Write' he was a somewhat precocious boy, writing his first poem at the age of four, his mother 'taking it down to dictation'. Being 'the middle of three', with an age gap of five years on either side between himself and his sisters, he was 'somewhat lonely'. 'I had', he continues, 'the lonely child's habit of making up stories and holding conversations with imaginary persons, and I think from the very start my literary ambitions were mixed up with the feelings of being isolated and undervalued.'

At the age of five he was sent to 'Sunnylands', a small Anglican convent school in Henley. Even at so young an age, he was to say, 'I knew that when I grew up I should be a writer.' Out of school the young Eric went for long walks, exploring the Oxfordshire countryside, gathering fruit from hedges with his mother according to the season, dewberries, blackberries, sloes, hazelnuts, beechnuts and crab-apples. At home the family kept an assortment of dogs, cats, rabbits and guinea pigs, and Orwell was to maintain a deep affection for animals all his life.

At the age of six he formed an infatuation with 'the plumber's daughter.' In the essay 'Such, Such Were the Joys', written in 1947 and published posthumously in 1952, he makes clear that the relationship was tinged with childish eroticism:

> At that time I was in an almost sexless state, which is normal, or at any rate common, in boys of that age; I was therefore in the position of simultaneously knowing and not knowing what used to be called the Facts of Life. At five or six, like many children I had passed through a phase of sexuality. My friends were the plumber's children up the road, and we used sometimes to play games of a vaguely erotic kind. One was called 'playing at doctors', and I remember getting a faint but definitely pleasant thrill from holding a toy trumpet, which was supposed to be a stethoscope, against a little girl's belly.

**Opposite** *'I was a chubby boy'. Like most young, middle-class boys in Edwardian England, the three-year-old Eric wore the obligatory sailor-suit.*

The association, however, was short-lived – the two were separated because Mrs Blair considered the plumber's daughter too 'common', and was afraid that her young son might, by associating with her, 'grow up with a vulgar accent.'

*Henley Regatta 1914, playground of the English upper classes. Orwell claimed to have become aware of English class divisions from an early age. Snobbery, he wrote, was a national characteristic, although it was 'mixed up with a kind of idealism, a feeling that style and tradition are more important than money'.*

Writing thirty years after the event in *The Road to Wigan Pier*, Orwell says that it was this experience which marked the time when 'the working class ceased to be a race of friendly and wonderful beings and became a race of enemies'. To the young Blair and 'to nearly all children of families' of his class, '"common" people seemed almost

sub-human'. It was to such opinions that Orwell attributed
the origins of 'a hatred of the working class' typical of his
class. At the root of this hatred was the belief 'summed up
in four frightful words which people nowadays are chary
of uttering, but which were bandied about quite freely in
my own childhood . . . *The lower classes smell.*'

As he grew older Orwell tended to look back nostalgically on Edwardian England, the period of his childhood, before the First World War (1914–18). As the narrator George Bowling in the novel *Coming Up For Air* (1939) remembers:

*Eric with his parents and younger sister Avril in 1916. Of himself at this age, Orwell wrote, 'I was weak, I was ugly, I was unpopular, I had a chronic cough, I was cowardly, I smelt'.*

. . . it was summer all year round. I'm quite aware that that's a delusion. I'm merely trying to tell you how things come back to me. If I shut my eyes and think of Lower Binfield any time before I was, say, eight, it's always in summer weather that I remember it. Either it's the market-place at dinner-time, with a sort of sleepy dusty hush over everything and the carrier's horse with his nose-bag, munching away, or it's a hot afternoon in the great green juicy meadows round the town, or it's about dusk in the lane behind the allotments, and there's a smell of pipe-tobacco and night-stocks floating through the hedge.

In *Coming Up For Air* 'Lower Binfield' is recognizably Henley-on-Thames and, like Orwell, George Bowling has a passion for coarse fishing. Looking back thirty years to his own childhood, Bowling asks:

> Where are the English coarse fish now? When I was a kid every pond and stream had fish in it. Now all the ponds are drained, and when the streams aren't poisoned with chemicals from factories they're full of rusty tins and motor-bike tyres.

The very names of the English coarse fish, 'roach, rudd, dace . . . chub, carp, tench' to Bowling are:

> . . . solid names. The people who made them up hadn't heard of machine-guns, they didn't live in terror of the sack or spend their time eating aspirins, going to the pictures, and wondering how to keep out of the concentration camp.

In stark contrast to the world Orwell was to create in *Nineteen Eighty-Four*, it was a safe, solid world that seemed as if it would last forever. But, as Orwell was to write in a review for the magazine *The Adelphi* in 1948, 'In many ways it is a grave handicap to remember that lost paradise "before the War" – that is, before the other war . . . ' Nor did Orwell entirely reject his early background and the beliefs associated with it. The 'early training in which the middle-class child is taught almost simultaneously to wash his neck and to die for his country' remained a strong conviction. As a writer he realized that he could not entirely escape from habits of thought formed as a child, even if he had wished to. Indeed, in the self-revealing essay 'Why I Write' he says that if the writer, any writer, 'escapes from his early influences altogether, he will have killed his impulse to write', and that in his own case, 'I am not able, and do not want, completely to abandon the world-view that I acquired in childhood'.

As his niece Jane Morgan was to say, Orwell retained many characteristics of his age and class:

> . . . I think a lot of Eric's hang-ups came from the fact that he thought he ought to love all his fellow-men; and he couldn't even talk to them easily. My father was the same sort of age and background and he could never speak to anyone without first placing them classwise.

*On holiday in Shropshire with Prosper and Guinever Buddicom, September 1917.*

Having spent the first eight years of his life almost exclusively in the company of women, Orwell's early childhood, his 'lost paradise', ended abruptly when he won a scholarship to St Cyprian's, an exclusive preparatory school on the Sussex Downs near Eastbourne. Here, in a virtually all-male world, he was to experience his first confrontation with hell.

# 2 The Best School of All

In 'Such, Such Were the Joys' (1947), Orwell describes his experiences 36 years earlier as a pupil at St Cyprian's preparatory school. His account reads like a horror story. 'Your home might be far from perfect, but it was at least a place ruled by love rather than fear', he wrote. 'At eight years old you were suddenly taken out of this warm nest and flung into a world of force and fraud and secrecy, like a gold-fish into a tank full of pike.'

The school was run on harsh, Spartan lines, a mixture of cold baths, insufficient food, severe punishment and bad teaching. Yet 'it was an expensive and snobbish school', attracting not only the sons of the prosperous middle-class, but also those of a sprinkling of aristocrats and South American millionaires. The appeal of St Cyprian's lay in the fact that it achieved a high success rate in getting its pupils through the Common Entrance examination, taken at the age of thirteen, and into the two top public schools, Eton and Harrow. But the school achieved such results by a mechanical form of instruction, and, if Orwell's account is true, capricious terror.

His start was not auspicious. 'Soon after I arrived at St Cyprian's . . . I began wetting my bed. I was now aged eight, so that this was a reversion to a habit which I must have grown out of at least four years earlier.' The bed-wetting filled him with shame. He came to dread nights, fearing a repetition of the event. 'Night after night I prayed, with a fervour never previously attained in my

*At the age of thirteen, Eric Blair entered Eton College, the most prestigious public school in England. After the intense effort needed to get into Eton, he felt he deserved a rest and was thought by his tutor to be 'always a bit of a slacker and a dodger', who did 'absolutely no work for five years'.*

prayers, "Please God, please do not let me wet my bed!", but it made remarkably little difference.' The bed-wetting persisted and Blair was ordered to report to the Headmaster, Mr Vaughan Wilkes. Nicknamed 'Sambo' by his pupils, Wilkes:

> . . . was a round-shouldered, curiously oafish-looking man, not large but shambling in gait, with a chubby face which was like that of an overgrown baby . . . He read me a short but pompous lecture, then seized me by the scruff of my neck, twisted me over and began beating me with a riding-crop. He had a habit of continuing his lecture while he flogged you, and I remember the words 'you dir-ty lit-tle boy' keeping time with the blows.

For telling another boy that the beating had not hurt, he was caned again, this time 'in real earnest'. He cried:

> ... because of a deeper grief which is peculiar to childhood and not easy to convey: a sense of desolate loneliness and helplessness, of being locked up not only in a hostile world but in a world of good and evil where the rules were such that it was actually not possible for me to keep them.

The idea that he was unable to keep to 'the rules' was to become a feature of his life. Almost from the beginning he viewed himself as an outsider. 'This was the great abiding lesson of my boyhood: that I was in a world where it was *not possible* for me to be good.'

*Eton College, 1921. Blair (second row, extreme right, seated by wall) thought Eton to be 'O.K.', 'tolerable' and 'all right'. In later life he was to praise the school for its 'tolerant and civilized atmosphere'.*

Although the older Orwell was to caution that, 'whoever writes about his childhood must beware of exaggeration and self-pity', the picture he paints of St Cyprian's in 'Such, Such Were the Joys' is one of almost unrelieved misery. The quality he was to identify as a unique feature of his writing, 'a power of facing unpleasant facts'', was given full rein in his essay on St Cyprian's. 'Once . . . a fair-haired boy had a choking fit at dinner, and a stream of snot ran out of his nose on to his plate, in a horrible way to see'.

Because he was taken by the school on reduced fees, Blair expected to work especially hard and bring credit to the school by winning a scholarship:

Very early it was impressed upon me that I had no chance of a decent future unless I won a scholarship at a public school. Either I won my scholarship, or I must leave school at fourteen and become in Sambo's favourite phrase 'a little office boy at forty pounds a year' . . . It is not easy to convey to a grown-up person the sense of strain, of nerving oneself for some terrible, all-deciding combat, as the date of the examination crept nearer.

To win his scholarship he was made to work, he later claimed, as he never worked again. If he slackened off or was inattentive Sambo goaded him: 'Go on you little slacker! Go on, you idle worthless boy! The trouble with you is that you're bone and horn idle. You eat too much, that's why . . . Go on, now, put your back into it. You're not *thinking*. Your brain doesn't sweat.'

Blair spent five years preparing for the two and a half days of examination, principally in Latin and Greek, 'crammed with learning as cynically as a goose is crammed for Christmas'. Despite his winning two scholarships, one at Wellington and the other at Eton, his time at St Cyprian's, he felt, marred him for much of his life. Such at any rate was the view of the mature Orwell. Certainly it is difficult to believe that at the age of twelve he already possessed the sophisticated awareness of class and the overwhelming power of money that were to be major themes of his later writing. But such was his claim. He was never allowed to forget, he said, the fact that he was a scholarship boy and that his parents were relatively poor. 'I never, for instance, succeeded in getting a cricket bat of my own because "Your parents wouldn't be able to afford it". This phrase pursued me throughout my schooldays.' The Headmaster's wife, nicknamed 'Flip', 'in particular, seemed to aim consciously at inculcating a humble outlook in the poorer boys . . . and she said this in front of the whole school: "You know you're not going to grow up with money, don't you? Your parents aren't rich. You must learn to be sensible. Don't get above yourself!"'

At the age of thirteen Eric Blair felt himself to be inferior to others. 'I had no money, I was weak, I was ugly, I was unpopular, I had a chronic cough, I was cowardly, I smelt.' Having been told this by his peers, he believed it to be true.

The conviction that it was *not possible* for me to be a success went deep enough to influence my actions till far into adult life. Until I was about thirty I always planned my life on the assumption not only that any major undertaking was

*An Eton Wall Game, 1921 (Eric Blair top left).*

**Opposite** *In a book of John Milton's poetry, Blair gave vent to his dislike of Milton's verse. The writers he most admired at the time were H.G. Wells, John Galsworthy and George Bernard Shaw.*

bound to fail, but that I could only expect to live a few years longer.

Blair left St Cyprian's at Christmas 1916 with an overwhelming sense of 'failure, failure, failure – failure behind me, failure ahead of me – that was the deepest conviction that I carried away.'

In 1917 he went to King's College, Eton, one of 70 scholars among 900 or so 'Oppidans' or non-scholarship boys. The mature Orwell praised Eton for its 'tolerant and civilized atmosphere', but said the school turned him into 'an odious little snob' although 'no worse than the other boys'. In *Twentieth Century Writers* (1942), he claimed: 'I don't feel that Eton has been much of a formative influence

E.A. Blair K.S.

Bought this Book

much against his will

For the study

of Milton,

a poet

for whom

he had

no

love;

but

he was

compelled

to study

him or abandon

English Extra Studies,

which not being

Commendable to him

He was compelled to

Squander three & sixpence

On this nasty little book.

25

in my life', and that he 'did no work . . . and learned very little'. After the effort of winning a scholarship to the school he took things easy. His tutor at College, A.S.F. Gower, thought of him as 'always a bit of a slacker and a dodger'.

In 'Why I Write' Orwell remembers that at the age of sixteen he 'discovered the joy of mere words, i.e. the sounds and associations of words. The lines from *Paradise Lost*:

> So hee with difficulty and labour hard
> Moved on: with difficulty and labour hee

which do not now seem to me so very wonderful, sent shivers down my backbone.' In that same essay he says that 'from an early age, perhaps the age of five or six, I knew that when I grew up I should be a writer'. His first published work, a patriotic poem entitled 'Awake! Young Men of England', appeared when he was eleven in September 1914 in the *Henley and South Oxfordshire Standard*. At Eton he wrote 'vers d'occasion, semi-comic poems' turning them out 'at astonishing speed', and at fourteen wrote 'a whole rhyming play, in imitation of Aristophanes, in about a week', in addition to helping to edit school magazines.

As at St Cyprian's, he felt himself to be different from other boys. George Wansborough, later a director of the Bank of England, remembered him as 'obviously a very different type of boy' from his contemporaries. He was reading widely and thinking critically about what he read. H.G. Wells was an important influence, as were George Bernard Shaw and John Galsworthy, 'at that time . . . regarded as "dangerously advanced" writers'. In *The Road to Wigan Pier* Orwell wrote that 'at the age of seventeen or eighteen, I was a snob and a revolutionary. I was against all authority . . . and . . . loosely described myself as a Socialist' although having 'not much grasp of what Socialism meant' and 'no notion that the working class were human beings'. While he could 'agonize over their sufferings' he 'still hated them and despised them when I came anywhere near them. I was still revolted by their accents and infuriated by their habitual rudeness'.

The degree to which he had slackened off at Eton became apparent during his final term. He was placed

*Frolicking on the banks of the River Thames at 'Athens', a well-known beauty spot close to Eton, in the summer of 1919.*

twelfth of the thirteen in his class. With no hope of obtaining a scholarship to Oxford he had to settle for a career. With his family background of service in India and Burma, the choice seemed obvious. For the Indian Civil Service, university-level qualifications were needed, so he opted for the Imperial Indian Police.

Eric Blair set sail for Burma, then an administrative sub-division of India, on 27 October 1922. He was nineteen years of age and a probationary Assistant Superintendent of Police. Burma had been taken over by Britain in 1885. When Blair arrived in 1922, resistance to British rule was simmering below the surface. There had been riots, local rebellions and demonstrations. As a policeman it was Blair's job to maintain law and order and to defuse any potential rebellion. 'I was in the police', he wrote in *The Road to Wigan Pier*, 'which is to say that I was part of the actual machinery of despotism.' He felt isolated and lonely, hated by the Burmese on the one hand and despising the English on the other. Like Flory, the central character in *Burmese Days* (1934), he came to feel that he was 'living a lie ... the lie that we're here to uplift our poor black brothers instead of to rob them'.

Blair was to spend 'five boring years' in Burma, 'within the sound of bugles'. After training at the Police School, Mandalay, he received his first posting in January 1924. A contemporary at Mandalay remembers him as 'a very pleasant fellow to know' although he 'kept very much to himself'. Unlike the other English policemen and officials he did not spend much time drinking at the Club. 'I don't think he went to the Club very much ... I think he mostly read ... or stayed up in his room.' Because of this he earned the reputation of being 'an eccentric'. He learned to speak Burmese fluently, played sport, read a great deal and did his job as best he could. But it was a job he came to hate. Nine years after leaving Burma he was to write, in *The Road to Wigan Pier*:

*In 1923, Blair (back row, third from left) was posted to the Police Training School at Mandalay, Burma. A contemporary at the school recalled him being 'good-looking, pleasant to talk to, easy of manner'.*

... in the police you see the dirty work of Empire at close quarters, and there is an appreciable difference between doing dirty work and merely profiting by it. Most people approve of capital punishment, but most people wouldn't

do the hangman's job. Even the other Europeans slightly looked down on the police because of the brutal work they had to do.

The 'brutal work' he witnessed affected him deeply. Because he was in some way 'directly responsible for them' he could not bear the sight of:

> . . . the wretched prisoners squatting in the reeking cages of the lock-ups, the grey cowed faces of the long-term convicts, the scarred buttocks of the men who had been flogged with bamboos, the women and children howling when their menfolk were led away under arrest.

He 'watched a man hanged once; it seemed to me worse than a thousand murders'. As he was to write in 'A Hanging' (1931):

> . . . till that moment I had never realized what it means to destroy a healthy, conscious man. When I saw the prisoner step aside to avoid the puddle I saw the mystery, the unspeakable wrongness, of cutting a life short when it is in full tide. This man was not dying, he was alive just as we are alive . . . and in two minutes . . . one of us would be gone – one mind less, one world less.

*Opposite The relationship between the white man serving the Empire and the subject black races became intolerable to Blair as his time in Burma went on. 'I perceived . . . that when the white man turns tyrant it is his own freedom that he destroys'.*

In *Burmese Days* (1934), his first published novel, Orwell explores the meaning of British rule in Burma. The novel does not merely expose the injustices perpetrated by the British upon innocent Burmese people, but shows how Empire-building – 'imperialism' – has a corrupting effect upon those called upon to administer the system. John Flory, the book's central character, is a dissolute 35-year-old timber merchant. Unloved, he can neither accept the narrow small-mindedness of the European community, centred on the Club and the appalling social-climber Mrs Lackersteen, nor feel much sympathy for those Burmese, like the scheming, corrupt U Po Kyin, who profit shamelessly from British rule. Nevertheless, Flory loves the country and traditional Burmese way of life. He falls in love with Elizabeth, Mrs Lackersteen's niece, but discovers her to be a shallow, bigoted philistine. The inherent racism of British rule is driven home to Flory when he attempts to make his Indian friend, Dr Veraswami, a member of the European Club. Incapable of

**Opposite** *Orwell in 1945 with a souvenir of his time in Burma.*

**Below** *Hunting, shooting and sport played an essential part of British social life in India and Burma. Blair, however, preferred to read and explore the Burmese countryside alone.*

changing the system or himself, yet unable to accept 'the slimy white man's burden humbug', at the end of the book Flory kills himself.

'Criminal law', wrote Orwell after leaving Burma, 'is a horrible thing. It needs very insensitive people to administer it'. Sensitive, isolated, lonely and shocked by the conduct of his fellow-Europeans, Blair had already decided to resign from the Indian Police when after five years he was sent home on leave. In an autobiographical sketch written in 1940 for an American publisher he wrote that he left the Indian Police 'partly because the climate had ruined my health, partly because I already had vague ideas of writing books, but mainly because I could not go on any longer serving an imperialism which I had come to regard as very largely a racket.'

# 3 Down and Out in Paris and London

Why did Eric Blair become a writer? In 'Why I Write' he claimed that:

> From an early age, perhaps the age of five or six, I knew that when I grew up I should be a writer. Between the ages of about seventeen and twenty-four I tried to abandon this idea, but I did so with the consciousness that I was outraging my true nature and that sooner or later I should have to settle down and write books.

Having decided to leave the Indian Police he turned his back on his upbringing, and despite having written nothing since the age of seventeen, and published nothing apart from a few adolescent poems, he became a writer. Writing in 1947, in 'Why I Write', Orwell assesses the reasons why anyone should wish to write and concludes that there are four basic motives – 'sheer egotism', 'aesthetic enthusiasm', 'historical impulse' and 'political purpose'. In his own case he was undoubtedly motivated, at least to begin with, by 'sheer egotism' – a 'desire to seem clever, to be talked about, to be remembered after death', and perhaps more importantly a desire 'to get your own back on grown-ups who snubbed you in childhood'. 'Aesthetic enthusiasm' was also an important motive. At first he wanted to write: 'enormous naturalistic novels with unhappy endings, full of detailed descriptions and arresting similes, and also full of purple passages in which

**Opposite** *The house in Notting Hill Gate, London, in which Blair rented a flat after his return from Burma.*

words were used partly for the sake of their sound'. Only later did an 'historical impulse' – a 'desire to see things as they are, to find out true facts and store them up for the use of posterity' – and 'political purpose' become the main motives for his writing.

Almost nothing that Blair wrote immediately after abandoning his career in the Imperial Indian Police has survived. A family friend, Ruth Pitter, who found him a room in London's Notting Hill soon after his return from Burma, remembers him *'trying* to write'. 'It didn't come easily', she recalls. 'At that time I don't think any of his friends believed he would ever write well. Indeed, I think he was unusually inept. We tried not to be discouraging, but we used to laugh till we cried at some bits he showed us . . . He wrote so badly. He had to teach himself how to write. He was like a cow with a musket . . . He became a master of English, but it was sheer hard grind.'

With little money, few friends and only a pile of rejection slips from publishers to show for his efforts, he had a hard time. Yet he was not unduly discouraged by failure. As he was to explain in *The Road to Wigan Pier*, the sense of failure he experienced during the years immediately following his return from Burma was important to his development both as a man and as a writer:

> I was conscious of an immense guilt that I had got to expiate . . . I felt that I had got to escape not merely from imperialism but from every form of man's dominion over man. I wanted to submerge myself, to get right down among the oppressed; to be one of them and on their side against the tyrants. And, chiefly because I had to think everything out in solitude, I carried my hatred of oppression to extraordinary lengths. At that time failure seemed to me to be the only virtue. Every suspicion of self-advancement, even to 'succeed' in life to the extent of making a few hundred pounds a year, seemed to me spiritually ugly, a species of bullying.

How far this was a rationalization of his failure as a writer is hard to say. He was drawn into poverty, or at least relative poverty, not only by a lack of money but also by a conscious desire to 'get right down among the oppressed':

> When I thought of poverty, I thought of it in terms of brute starvation. Therefore my mind turned immediately

**Opposite** *The collapse of the international money market on Wall Street, New York, in 1929 had a profound effect worldwide. In Britain, mass unemployment, never before experienced, meant that many, such as this unemployed coalminer from Wigan in Lancashire, suffered poverty and a sense of hopelessness for a decade.*

37

towards the extreme cases, the social outcasts: tramps, beggars, criminals, prostitutes. These were 'the lowest of the low', and these were the people with whom I wanted to get into contact. What I profoundly wanted, at that time, was to find some way of getting out of the respectable world altogether.

To accomplish this he went into a second-hand clothes shop and bought a set of ragged clothes. As he reported in his first published major work *Down and Out in Paris and London* (1933):

> My new clothes . . . put me instantly into a new world. Everyone's demeanour seemed to have changed abruptly. I helped a hawker pick up a barrow that he had upset. 'Thanks, mate,' he said with a grin. No one had called me mate before in my life – it was the clothes that had done it.

Dressed in ragged clothes he set out one winter's night for Limehouse, one of the poorest districts in the East End of London. As he entered a common lodging-house: 'a dark, dirty-looking place', a drunken stevedore (dock worker) lurched towards him. Fearing assault:

> I stiffened myself. So the fight was coming already! The next moment the stevedore collapsed on my chest and flung his arms round my neck. 'Ave a cup of tea, chum! he cried tearfully; 'ave a cup of tea!' . . . It was a kind of baptism.

**Opposite** *Two unemployed workers share a cigarette, Wigan 1939. What Orwell saw during his visit to Wigan in 1936 shocked him and confirmed his belief in the necessity of socialism.*

**Below** *Known as 'Chinatown', Limehouse was one of the poorest districts in the East End of London.*

*A soup kitchen in London in the 1920s. For the homeless these kitchens, run by charitable and religious organizations, provided what was often the only food available for 'the lowest of the low'.*

Blair made several excursions of this kind into the East End during the winter of 1928–9. The experience did much to shape his views on class and power. 'Why do tramps exist at all?' he asks in *Down and Out in Paris and London*. 'Curiously, few people know that a tramp takes to the road not because he likes it, but because there happens to be a law compelling him to do so. A destitute man can only find relief at casual wards [called 'spikes'] and since each spike will admit him for only one night, he is automatically kept moving.'

As Blair was to discover, spikes were run on principles little changed since the nineteenth century. Tobacco was forbidden, but 'since we knew that the porter never searched below the knee, we hid our tobacco in our boots.' There was also the feeling that the tramps should work for their keep. 'The work was peeling potatoes for dinner – but it was a mere formality, to keep us occupied.' But what angered him most were the shelters run by the Salvation Army. In these he was made to feel grateful for the charity handed out. In one such shelter he overheard two tramps:

> 'You 'ad your bun', said one; 'you got to pay for it'. 'Pray for it, you mean. They can't give you a cup of tea without you go down on your . . . knees for it.'

With what was left of his meagre savings he moved to Paris in the spring of 1929. There he could live more cheaply than in London, learn French, earn some extra money as an English tutor if need be and absorb the cosmopolitan atmosphere of the French capital – the haunt in the 1920s of such writers as Scott Fitzgerald, Ernest Hemingway and James Joyce. He took a room in a cheap

*In the 1920s, Paris became the centre of literary and cultural innovation and was the home of James Joyce (second from left), author of* Ulysses, *a book which revolutionized the form and structure of the novel. In the spring of 1929 Blair moved to Paris to live more cheaply and to write.*

hotel in the Rue du Pot de Fer. The district was not 'a representative Paris slum' as he was to claim, but, according to Hemingway 'the best [that is, the most typical] part of the Latin Quarter', inhabited by Algerians, foreign workers, and a shifting population of unemployed. There he wrote two novels which were never published and which were subsequently either lost or destroyed. He contributed an article to *Le Monde*; several pieces, including one on Burma, to the radical newspaper *Progrès Civique* and to *G.K.'s Weekly* in England. But overwork, underfeeding and the cold took their toll and in February 1929 he was admitted to the Hôpital Cochin with pneumonia. His harrowing experience in hospital is described in the documentary short story 'How the Poor Die', written seventeen years later in 1946.

By the summer of 1929, 'almost penniless and in urgent need of a job', he decided that it was 'more sensible' to stay in Paris 'rather than go back to England where there were then about two and half million unemployed'. Robbed of his remaining savings he was forced to take any job he could find, and eventually did so as a *plongeur* or dish-washer in the kitchen of a fashionable hotel, working thirteen hours a day for very low wages. In *Down and Out in Paris and London* Orwell recounts the life of the typical *plongeur*:

> A *plongeur* is better off than many manual workers, but still, is no freer than if he were bought and sold. His work is servile and without art; he is paid just enough to keep him alive; his only holiday is the sack. Except by a lucky chance, he has no escape from this life, save into prison. If *plongeurs* thought at all, they would strike for better treatment. But they do not think; they have no leisure for it.

**Opposite** *Ernest Hemingway with friends in Paris. He lived among the American literary group in Paris during the time when Blair – an unknown and unpublished author – was working washing dishes in a fashionable restaurant.*

Blair worked as a *plongeur* for ten weeks. With five pounds sent to him by an English friend he returned 'home' to his parents' house at Southwold on the Suffolk coast for Christmas 1929. Eighteen months in Paris had changed him. Although not yet a socialist he had come to reject the society in which he had been brought up. In his view it was based on nothing more noble than money and commercial exploitation. His writing was evolving towards the crisp, direct and colloquial style that was to

On Southwold Beach, Suffolk. After suffering a breakdown in health and a period in hospital (described in 'How the Poor Die'), Eric Blair returned to his parents' home in Southwold.

characterize his later work. It was a style he regarded at the time as journalistic, not literary, and he continued to write 'naturalistic novels . . . full of detailed descriptions . . . and . . . purple passages'. Despite disappointment, rejection, poor health and poverty he was pursuing his craft with single-minded determination.

# 4 Becoming George Orwell

The years Eric Blair spent on the 'fringe of poverty' taught him 'one or two things' that helped him overcome some of the prejudices he had acquired in his boyhood and youth. 'I shall never again think that all tramps are drunken scoundrels', he writes in *Down and Out in Paris and London*, 'nor expect a beggar to be grateful when I give him a penny, nor be surprised if men out of work lack energy, nor subscribe to the Salvation Army, nor pawn my clothes, nor refuse a handbill, nor enjoy a meal in a smart restaurant. That is a beginning.'

From such a beginning Eric Blair was to become 'George Orwell', novelist, journalist, democratic socialist, commentator on his times. The transition was neither easy nor planned. As in the past, he was beset by failure and disappointment. But by 1936, when he went to fight on the Republican side in the Spanish Civil War (1936-9), George Orwell was an established, if somewhat minor writer and Eric Blair, old Etonian, ex-Assistant Superintendent of Police, was long forgotten.

Money, as always, was a problem. Taking to the road soon after his return from Paris, he roamed Kent, where he went hop-picking; as well as Bedfordshire and Essex, and concluded that:

> Tramps are not really dirty as English people go, but they have the name of being dirty, and when you have shared a bed with a tramp and drunk tea out of the same snuff-tin, you feel you have seen the worst and the worst has no terrors for you.

*Hop-picking in Kent attracted many of London's East Enders, as well as gypsies and tramps.*

**Opposite** *By 1932 the Depression had worsened and in New York the long line of the unemployed queuing for bread became a familiar sight.*

Even for those living only on 'the fringe of poverty' they were hard times. The Wall Street Crash in 1929 led to economic recession in the USA, Britain and Europe, and to mass unemployment. Democratic governments were unable to cope with the collapse of the world financial order. In Britain a Labour Government elected in 1929 seemingly gave up its principles for financial orthodoxy and by 1931 had been replaced by a National Government led by the ex-Labour Prime Minister Ramsay MacDonald. Unemployment continued to rise, social security benefits were cut and a means test introduced to establish who was still eligible for them, and real poverty was experienced by millions of workers for the first time.

LINE FOR
1₵ RESTAURANT
20 MEALS FOR 1₵
DONATIONS INVITED
HELP FEED THE HUNGRY
I WILL FEED 20
1₵ RESTAURANT
107 W. 43rd ST.

*The inability of political parties to cope with the financial crisis led to the creation of extremist parties of both left and right throughout Europe. In Britain, Sir Oswald Mosley formed the British Union of Fascists in 1933. Mosley is seen here at a fascist rally held in the Albert Hall, London, in 1934.*

In such conditions political extremism flourished. Following the election of Adolf Hitler in Germany as head of a National Socialist (Nazi) dictatorship in 1933, the ex-Labour minister Sir Oswald Mosley formed the British Union of Fascists. Others looked to Soviet Russia as a way out of the mess. Membership of the British Communist Party, particularly among privileged young under-graduates at the universities of Oxford and Cambridge, increased. There were mass demonstrations, hunger marches and social unrest.

Writing as furiously as ever, book reviews, articles, poems, a novel (*Burmese Days*), but unable to get *Down and Out in Paris and London* published – it was rejected by T.S. Eliot on behalf of the publishers Faber & Faber – Blair needed money in order to live. He was at a low ebb, living

in a bug-infested 'filthy kip' at Westminster Chambers in south-east London, which became the model for the 'frowsy attic' inhabited by Gordon Comstock, the embittered, struggling poet in *Keep the Aspidistra Flying* (1936). Clearly he needed a job. In the new year of 1932 he took up an appointment as Headmaster at a school of sixteen boys called The Hawthornes at Hayes in Middlesex. It was the kind of third-rate private school he was to satirize in *A Clergyman's Daughter* (1935). Despite the unpromising circumstances, Blair took teaching seriously. 'No job is more fascinating . . . if you have a free hand at it – though if you are forced to bore your pupils and oppress them, they will hate you for it.' One old boy remembers him as being a strict disciplinarian, keeping a large stick by his desk, which he 'used fairly often'. But he was respected and liked because he 'seemed to think of the boys as friends'.

*Demonstrators protest against the cut in unemployment benefit, Hyde Park, London, 30 September 1931. The political, social and literary life of England during the 1930s came to be dominated by the problem of unemployment.*

Unknown to Blair, the manuscript of *Down and Out in Paris and London*, given to a friend to destroy, was sent to the literary agent Leonard Moore, who offered it to the publisher Victor Gollancz. It was accepted, subject to revision. To his agent Blair wrote, 'see that it is published pseudonymously, as I am not very proud of it'. The pseudonyms he suggested were P. S. Burton, 'a name I always use when tramping', 'Kenneth Miles, George Orwell, H. Lewis Allways. I rather favour George Orwell', he added. So did Gollancz. Thus 'George Orwell' was born.

Published in January 1933, the book was generally well-received by reviewers, but sold only modestly and not well enough for Orwell to give up 'foul teaching'. Leaving The Hawthornes he took another teaching job at Frays College, Uxbridge, a larger private boarding school, while completing *Burmese Days*. He remained at Frays College only one term. In December he caught a chill which developed into pneumonia and was rushed into Uxbridge Cottage Hospital. He was very ill. His parents, anxious about his health, urged him to give up teaching and stay with them in Southwold. To Orwell it must have

*Teaching at The Hawthornes School, Hayes, Middlesex, 1933, the year in which* Down and Out in Paris and London *was published.*

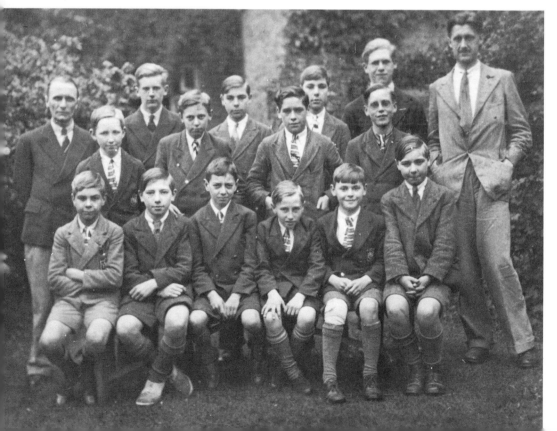

been a blessing in disguise since, as he wrote to Moore, it meant he was 'able to write my next novel'.

The new novel was to be called *A Clergyman's Daughter* (1935) and tells the story of Dorothy Hare, the twenty-eight-year-old unmarried daughter of the self-absorbed Reverend Charles Hare. Her life is dull, repetitive, hard-working and empty of meaning. She is sexually frigid and shies away from men. She has also, although she refuses to admit it to herself at the beginning of the book, lost her religious faith – the only thing that gives shape to her life. An accident that occurs in the house of her free-thinking, worldly friend Mr Warburton results in a loss of memory. Mysteriously she finds herself in London. Penniless and friendless, she meets up with a group of down-and-outs and goes hop-picking with them in Kent. The descriptions of impoverished London life, hop-picking, the suffocating respectability of Dorothy's 'genteel poor' existence in a country town and the grim private school in a London suburb where she teaches, are all drawn from Orwell's own experiences.

*Montague House, Suffolk. Having abandoned teaching because of poor health, Orwell lived here with his parents during 1934 and wrote* A Clergyman's Daughter.

Completing the novel in October 1934, he found a part-time job in a bookshop, 'Booklover's Corner' in Hampstead, north London. As in his earlier books, Orwell was to use this period of his life as the basis for his next novel, *Keep the Aspidistra Flying* (1936). Gordon Comstock, 'last member of the Comstock family, aged twenty-nine and rather moth-eaten already', is an aspiring poet who has given up a 'good' job as a copywriter for an advertising agency in order to write. But poverty prevents him from attaining the peace of mind he needs in order to write.

*Orwell at work. In* Keep the Aspidistra Flying *he wrote about the problems of an aspiring writer.*

Self-pitying, embittered, like Flory in *Burmese Days* and later Winston Smith in *Nineteen Eighty-Four*, Comstock feels himself to be essentially unlovable. He rails against the 'money-god' who rules almost every aspect of modern life. Of one of the characters in the novel Comstock reflects:

He had a sort of charm, a glamour, like all moneyed people. Money and charm; who shall separate them? If you have no money, men won't care for you, women won't love you. Moneyless, you are unlovable. Give me not righteousness, O Lord, give me money, only money.

Lonely and self-absorbed, he lives a hand-to-mouth existence in seedy digs, worrying about whether he can pay the rent and irritable because he never has enough money to smoke as much as he would wish.

Although it rails against the 'money-god', *Keep the Aspidistra Flying* is not a political novel. Comstock's revolt against society is personal. He despises those who seek a political change in society almost as much as he despises those engaged in the money-grubbing rat race. But Orwell's attack on the 'money-god' is not only directed at the way it forces people into economic servitude. It also distorts the relations between men and women. When Gordon falls in love with Rosemary he feels unable to consummate their relationship because of a lack of money. Afraid of making Rosemary pregnant because he is too poor to marry her and support a family, he is nevertheless unwilling to use contraceptives. In the end, seduced by Rosemary, Comstock gives up poetry for his old job as a copywriter in order to marry her and raise the child she is expecting. They move into a modest flat and as an act of contrition Gordon buys an aspidistra, symbol of middle-class respectability. But he accepts defeat with some degree of dignity. He sees that although 'our civilisation is founded on greed and fear . . . in the lives of common men the greed and fear are mysteriously transmuted into something nobler'. Like Comstock, Orwell was beginning to see 'in the lives of common men' a vision of society which gave hope for a better future.

In January 1936, soon after finishing *Keep the Aspidistra Flying*, Orwell was commissioned by Gollancz to write a book about working-class life in the north of England. He set out almost immediately. The journey, which lasted two

*The depressed industrial landscape of Wigan, Lancashire, where Orwell lived for a few weeks during 1936, collecting material for his book on the condition of the working class in the north of England,* The Road to Wigan Pier.

months, was to cement his growing political commitment and result in *The Road to Wigan Pier* (1937), which established his reputation as a political writer.

*The Road to Wigan Pier* is a mixture of reportage, documentary, observation, comment and polemic. The first part is a fairly straightforward account of working-class life in Wigan, Barnsley and Sheffield in the north of England. It opens in a tripe shop where Orwell lodged for several weeks. It was a dirty, smelly, run-down place described in the manner he had used to describe low-life in Paris:

> Downstairs there was the usual kitchen living-room with its huge open range burning night and day . . . In front of the fire there was always a line of damp washing, and in the middle of the room was the big kitchen table at which

the family and all the lodgers ate. I never saw this table completely uncovered, but I saw its various wrappings at different times. At the bottom there was a layer of old newspaper stained by Worcester Sauce; above that a sheet of sticky white oil-cloth; above that a green serge cloth; above that a coarse linen cloth, never changed and seldom taken off. Generally the crumbs from breakfast were still on the table at supper. I used to get to know individual crumbs by sight and watch their progress up and down the table from day to day.

After a few weeks spent in Wigan, Orwell moved on to a coal-mining community. As 'the train bore me away, through the monstrous scenery of slag-heaps, chimneys, piled scrap-iron, foul canals, paths of cindery mud criss-crossed by the print of clogs', he witnessed a scene

*Rows of back-to-back terrace houses, in Middlesborough, similar to the miners' cottages in Wigan.*

he was to turn into one of the most vivid pieces he ever wrote about the degrading effects of poverty:

*Miners hacking coal from a seam in typically cramped conditions. The working face at the mine visited by Orwell at Wigan was only 66 cm high.*

As we moved slowly through the outskirts of the town we passed row after row of little grey slum houses running at right angles from the embankment. At the back of one of the houses a young woman was kneeling on the stones, poking a stick up a leaden waste-pipe which ran from the sink inside and which I supposed was blocked. I had time to see everything about her – her sacking apron, her clumsy clogs, her arms reddened by the cold. She looked up as the train passed, and I was almost near enough to catch her eye. She had a round pale face, the usual exhausted face of a slum girl who is twenty-five and looks forty, thanks to miscarriage and drudgery; and it wore, for the second in which I saw it, the most desolate, hopeless expression I have ever seen. It struck me that we are mistaken when we say that 'It isn't the same for them as it would be for us', and that people bred in the slums can imagine nothing but slums. For what I saw in her face was not the ignorant suffering of an animal. She knew well enough what was happening to her – understood it as well as I did how dreadful a destiny it was to be kneeling there in the bitter cold, on the slimy stones of a slum backyard, poking a stick up a foul drain-pipe.

The writing is simple, matter-of-fact, yet sympathetic. Orwell feels that he understands the young woman's plight, not as a detached observer but from her own point of view. Visiting a coal-face was 'like hell, or at any rate like my own mental picture of hell. Most of the things one imagines in hell are there – heat, noise, confusion, darkness, foul air, and, above all, unbearably cramped space.' The miners, with their 'wide shoulders tapering to slender supple waists, and small pronounced buttocks and sinewy thighs', filled him with admiration and led him to reflect that 'the miner's job would be as much beyond my power as it would be to perform on the flying trapeze or to win the Grand National'.

*Miners returning home from work, Wigan, 1939. Orwell noted that 'the miner's job would be as much beyond my power as it would be to perform on the flying trapeze or to win the Grand National'.*

57

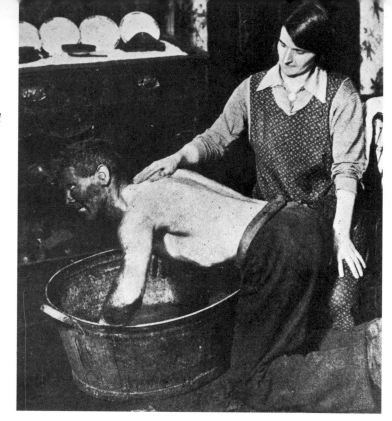

*With no bathrooms and no washing facilities at the mine, miners were scrubbed down by their wives in a tin bath in the main living room at home.*

For those in employment, Orwell noted a decency and contentment in their home life that he had never seen in a middle-class home:

> In a working class home . . . you breathe a warm, decent, deeply human atmosphere which it is not so easy to find elsewhere. I should say that a manual worker, if he is in steady work and drawing good wages . . . has a better chance of being happy than an 'educated' man. His home life seems to fall more naturally into a sane and comely shape . . . Especially on winter evenings after tea, when the fire glows in the open range . . . when Father, in shirt-sleeves, sits in the rocking chair at one side of the fire reading the racing finals, and Mother sits on the other side with her sewing, and the children are happy with a pennyworth of mint humbugs, and the dog lolls roasting himself on the rag mat . . .

**Opposite** *'Housing conditions in Wigan', noted Orwell on 13 February 1936, 'terrible. Mrs H. tells me that at her brother's house 11 people, 5 of them adults, belonging to 3 different families, live in 4 rooms, '2 up 2 down'.*

In the second part of *The Road to Wigan Pier*, Orwell gives a biographical description of his life prior to his visit to the north of England, which he saw as a turning point. If he had flirted with socialism before his journey, he came back

The confrontation
between Mosley's
fascists and the
Communist Party
in London in 1936
became known as the
Battle of Cable Street.

**Below** *Eileen
O'Shaughnessy,
Orwell's first wife.*

convinced of its necessity. Yet, he asks, why do so few people want socialism when they have so much to gain by it? The answer, he says, is that there is something deeply repugnant about socialists themselves. To Orwell and, he suspects, to most ordinary 'decent' working men, the word 'socialist' conjures up an image of 'fruit-juice drinkers, nudists, sandal-wearers, sex-maniacs, Quakers, "Nature Cure" quacks, pacifists and feminists . . . who come flocking towards the smell of "progress" like blue-bottles to a dead cat.' Unfair, no doubt, but the passage marks the beginning of his crusade to purge socialism of what he saw as hypocrisy, humbug and cant in order that ordinary people should see that its essential virtues – freedom and equality – are worth achieving.

Orwell wrote *The Road to Wigan Pier* during the summer and autumn of 1936 in a small cottage at Wallington in Hertfordshire which he rented soon after his return from the north of England. Now married to Eileen O'Shaughnessy – about whom, after only one meeting, he confided to a friend, 'Now *that* is the kind of girl I would like to marry' – he opened a general store in the front room of the cottage, bought a bacon slicer and sold sweets to the village children. Although not a great commercial success, the shop made enough to pay the weekly rent. In the large garden at the back of the cottage he grew vegetables and kept chickens and geese. He later acquired a goat which he milked religiously at first light. Writing in the morning, he ran the shop in the afternoons. It was, said a friend, probably the happiest time of his life.

# 5

# Spain

The happiness was to be short-lived. In December 1936 Orwell set off for Spain. His reason for going, he told a friend, was to 'kill fascists . . . After all, there are not such a terrific lot of fascists in the world: if we each shot one of them . . . '

In July 1936 civil war had broken out in Spain when General Franco staged a military coup to topple the democratically-elected government – a coalition of liberals, socialists, anarchists and communists – by force. The government, aided by a spontaneous demonstration of popular support, resisted and Spain was plunged into a bloody civil war that was to last three years. To those on the political left in Europe, Spain became the symbol of the struggle between fascism and democracy.

*The revolt by the Spanish army in Morocco led by General Franco (centre), against the Spanish government, led to a civil war that was to ravage Spain and divide Europe for three years.*

*Faced with Franco's insurrection, the disparate forces of the Spanish Republic rallied to its defence. Here volunteers – note their casual dress and lack of uniform – leave for the battle front in the Guadarrama Mountains.*

In fact the issues were not so clear-cut. For, while actively supported by arms and men from Fascist Italy and Nazi Germany, Franco was not himself a fascist. He wished Spain to remain an almost feudal state, ruled by 'strong' authoritarian government allied to the Catholic Church and rich land-owners. On the government side all was confusion. Liberals and moderate socialists wanted Spain to be a modern, parliamentary democracy. In this, strangely, they were supported by the pro-Russian Communist Party, which argued that this was the best way of uniting the anti-Franco forces and securing victory. The Anarchists, on the other hand, supported by anti-Russian communists, wanted to create a revolution at the same time as defeating Franco. In-fighting between these groups soon became as much an issue as defeating Franco. Into this cauldron of conflict George Orwell unwittingly stepped in December 1936.

In *Homage to Catalonia* (1938), the book he wrote about his experiences in Spain on his return to England in 1937, Orwell describes how Barcelona at that time, where the Anarchists were in control, had been turned into a sort of workers' state:

> In outward appearance it was a town in which the wealthy classes had practically ceased to exist. Except for a small number of women and foreigners there were no 'well-dressed' people at all. Practically everyone wore rough working-class clothes, or blue overalls, or some variant of military uniform. All this was queer and moving. There was much in it that I did not understand, in some ways I did not even like it, but I recognized it immediately as a state of affairs worth fighting for . . . Above all there was a belief in the revolution and the future, a feeling of suddenly having emerged into an era of equality and freedom. Human beings were trying to behave as human beings and not cogs in the capitalist machine.

*Spectators at a bullfight in Seville raise their arms in the fascist salute. Franco attracted the support of the Spanish fascists, rich landowners and the Catholic Church.*

63

*A reunion of British I.L.P. members who had fought in Spain – Letchworth, Hertfordshire, 1937. Orwell is second from the left.*

Armed with letters of introduction from the British Independent Labour Party (I.L.P.), Orwell (under the name of Eric Blair) enlisted in the militia of the P.O.U.M., a left-wing socialist party, and the I.L.P.'s sister organization in Spain. As an ex-Etonian officer cadet and policeman in Burma, he was put in charge of 50 young, tough, undisciplined Catalonians, instructing them in the rudiments of military drill. It was a ramshackle army, poorly trained, equipped only with an assortment of out-of-date weapons, but enthusiastic and full of revolutionary fervour. Posted to the Aragon front at Alcubierre, 320 km west of Barcelona, Orwell arrived in January 1937 in bitterly cold weather. Approaching the front he experienced for the first time 'the characteristic smell of war – a smell of excrement and decaying food'. In a quiet section of the line he suffered more from bronchitis, brought on by the cold, than from any enemy fire. The two opposing sides faced each other from trenches hastily dug the previous October. 'In trench warfare five things are important', he noted in *Homage to Catalonia*, 'firewood, food, tobacco, candles and the enemy. In winter . . . they were important in that order.'

Orwell spent five months on the Aragon front. The reality of war, a combination of boredom, discomfort and fear, is brilliantly conveyed in *Homage to Catalonia*, the most straightforwardly factual of all his books, combining biography with an overall analysis of the war and political situation in Spain. Regarded by some as his best book, simply but effectively written, *Homage to Catalonia* fulfils exactly the ideal that Orwell was later to regard as the essence of a good writer. 'The first thing that we ask of a writer', he says in 'Why I Write', 'is that he shall not tell us lies, that he shall say what he really thinks, what he really feels'. Honestly stating what he felt to be true, the book chronicles Orwell's growing disillusionment at the way the war was conducted and, more importantly for his future development as a writer, his first-hand experience of the problems of a certain brand of communism.

*In March 1937 Eileen Blair (crouching) visited her husband (tall figure in centre) on the Aragon front near Huesca, Spain.*

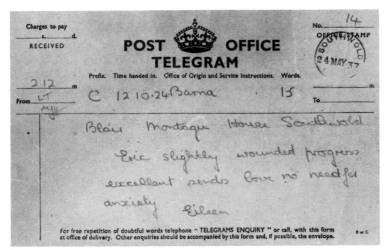

*When Orwell was hit by a sniper's bullet through the throat, his wife sent a telegram to his parents in Southwold. Characteristically, she made light of his condition. In fact Orwell was lucky to have survived.*

On leave in Barcelona in May with his wife, who had gone to Spain to join him and work as a secretary in the I.L.P. office in Barcelona, Orwell was approached by a friend in the hotel he was staying at and told: 'There's been some kind of trouble at the Telephone Exchange'. Only later did he learn that street-fighting had broken out between the Anarchists and the Communist-backed Civil Guard. Claiming that the Anarchists – with whom the P.O.U.M. sided – were secretly allied to the fascists, the Communist Party were attempting to crush all opposition and establish one-party control of Barcelona. At first Orwell did not understand what the fighting was about. As the historian Raymond Carr was to observe: 'Orwell was affected less by the May fighting than by the ruthless use the Communists made of a political post-mortem in order to destroy their enemies'. As he was later to discover, the Communists' version of events was widely reported in England as the true state of affairs. After five months fighting fascists with the P.O.U.M., Orwell understandably felt outraged. It was his first experience of how history could be re-written – a major theme of *Nineteen Eighty-Four*.

Ten days after returning to the front near Huesca, Orwell was shot through the neck, just under the larynx, by a single sniper's bullet. 'My first thought', he recalled, 'conventionally enough, was for my wife. My second was a violent resentment at having to leave this world which, when all is said and done, suits me so well'. Had the bullet

**Opposite** *A Spanish anti-fascist poster in which fascism is shown as an 'angel of death'. The swastika symbolizes the involvement of Nazi Germany on the side of Franco, and the rosary the support of the Catholic church.*

been a millimetre to the left he would have been killed. Recovering, he returned to Barcelona to be met by his anxious wife.

The Anarchists, P.O.U.M. and their foreign supporters had by now been declared illegal. Party activists were being rounded up and flung into gaol. It was time for the Orwells to get out. But before they left, risking arrest, they tried to secure the release of a friend. It was a foolhardy act but one which Sir Richard Rees, a friend from the early 1930s, described as typical of the Orwells' 'extraordinary courage and selflessness'.

*Orwell writing at the villa he rented in Marrakech from September 1938 to March 1939. It was here that he wrote* Coming Up For Air.

Hounded by the Communists, the Orwells safely crossed the frontier into France a few days later. Back in the cottage at Wallington in July, Orwell immediately started work on *Homage to Catalonia*, in which he described how the revolution was betrayed – a theme he was to return to in *Animal Farm*. While the Communists in Spain were claiming to be defending democracy and fighting for a social revolution, in reality , as Orwell wrote to a friend: 'The grotesque feature, which very few people outside Spain have yet grasped, is that the Communists . . . were more anxious even than the liberals to hunt down the revolutionaries and stamp out all revolutionary ideas'.

In the new year 1938 Orwell finished *Homage to Catalonia*, wrote book reviews because he needed the money, and began thinking about a new novel. In March a tubercular lesion he had developed bled and, seriously ill, he entered a sanatorium in Kent. His typewriter was taken from him and he was advised to cut down on his heavy smoking. By September he was well enough to set sail with his wife for Morocco to recuperate. Renting a small villa in Marrakech, he settled down to write his new novel, *Coming Up For Air*.

The novel, regarded by many as his most accomplished, tells the story of George Bowling, a 'five pounds a week' insurance agent with 'a house in the suburbs'. Fat, red-faced, middle-aged, with a nagging wife and two whinging kids he is almost a comic postcard caricature. Despite this appearance, Bowling is intelligent and deeply aware of the age in which he lives. In his homely style he sees through 'all the smelly little orthodoxies which are now contending for our souls', as Orwell described in his essay 'Charles Dickens' (1939). And the book is a warning of what is to come: the society of *Nineteen Eight-Four*, unless something is done to stop it:

> The . . . hate-world, slogan world. The coloured shirts. The barbed wire. The rubber truncheons. The secret cells where the light burns night and day and the detective watching you while you sleep. And the processions and the posters with enormous faces, and the crowds of a million people all cheering the leader till they deafen themselves into thinking that they really worship him, and all the time, underneath, they hate him so that they want to puke. It's all going to happen. Or isn't it? Some days I know it's impossible, other days I know it's inevitable.

Bowling, of course, knows that it was happening in Hitler's Germany and Stalin's USSR. Could it happen in England? Old England, which Bowling associates with his childhood in the market town of Lower Binfield, has already been destroyed by the twin evils, industrialism and capitalism. Revisiting the town, he finds it changed out of recognition. A housing estate stands where once there was an undiscovered carp lake. Roads and the motor car have destroyed the old market-place. Even the beer is not what it used to be, polluted by chemicals which give

*Adolf Hitler, dictator of Nazi Germany, attends a rally in 1938. The threat posed by Hitler's Germany dominated international politics from the mid-1930s. By 1938 war between Britain and Germany seemed inevitable.*

him a stomachache and hangover. And overshadowing it all is the terrible knowledge that within a year or two the safe, solid world of the nine-to-fivers is all going to be smashed to smithereens by aerial bombing and the establishment of the 'hate world'. 'I'll tell you what my stay in Lower Binfield has taught me', says George Bowling, 'and it is this':

It's all going to happen. All the things you've got at the back of your mind, the things that you're terrified of, the things you tell yourself are just a nightmare or only happen in foreign countries. The bombs, the food-queues, the rubber truncheons, the barbed wire, the coloured shirts, the slogans, the enormous faces, the machine-guns squirting out of bedroom windows. It's all going to happen . . . There's no escape. Fight against it if you like, or look the other way and pretend not to notice, grab your spanner and rush out to do a bit of face-smashing along with the others. But there's no way out. It's just something that's got to happen.

*While war clouds loomed over Europe in the autumn of 1938, a cordon of policemen separate fascists and anti-fascists in London's Trafalgar Square. As Orwell noted, ironically it was the Left, who for years had advocated peace and disarmament, who were now calling for war.*

*During the Munich crisis of 1938, when Britain almost went to war over the annexation by Germany of part of Czechoslovakia, gas masks were issued to the civilian population in Britain, including toddlers and babies. When war came, though, the fear that gas bombs would be dropped on London proved to have been unfounded.*

In the same mood George Orwell wrote to a friend in January 1939: 'We may get home just in time to go straight into the concentration camp if we haven't been sunk by a German submarine . . . I trust when next we meet it won't be behind barbed wire'.

Although deeply pessimistic, *Coming Up For Air* has some hope in it. The celebration of the English countryside – what was left of it – of fishing, of Bowling's common-sense, no-nonsense, essentially tolerant point of view, all give some cause for hope and reason for living.

While the Orwells were in Morocco, events on the world stage were moving closer to war. Shortly after they left England in the autumn of 1938, war between Britain and Germany was averted only when the British Prime Minister, Neville Chamberlain, virtually handed Czechoslovakia to Hitler on a plate. At the end of March the war in Spain ended with victory for Franco. In London the parks were dug up for air-raid shelters, gas-masks issued and plans for the evacuation of children from cities finalized. When the arch-enemies Nazi Germany and the Communist USSR signed the non-aggression pact in August 1939, in which they agreed to divide Poland between them, war was inevitable.

# 6 Wartime London

The beginning of the Second World War after Hitler invaded Poland in 1939, was a frustrating time for Orwell. With his paramilitary experience in Burma and service in

*In the months following the declaration of war on Germany in September 1939, almost a quarter of London's population fled for the safety of the countryside. Characteristically, the Orwells left their country cottage and returned to London.*

*The evacuation of women and children from London began on 1 September 1939. By the evening of 3 September, only hours after the declaration of war, one-and-a-half million had left London and were settled in the country.*

the Spanish Civil War he felt uniquely qualified to undertake an active part in the fighting. Despite repeated efforts to join up, however, he was turned down on the grounds of poor health. With censorship and paper rationing there were fewer outlets for his journalism, and the circumstances, he felt, were not right for writing novels. However, the war taught him something about himself he had not known: that he was a patriot and that there were things about England that he felt were worth fighting for.

He had not always felt so. Indeed, almost up to the declaration of war he had taken the view that conflict between England and Germany would be 'imperialist', a war fought between two competing commercial nations interested only in securing their overseas markets. But when war came in 1939 he saw that the defeat of Hitler was necessary if democratic socialism was to survive. He also believed, rather fancifully, that the war would lead to social revolution in England. Orwell, wrote Cyril Connolly, a friend since his schooldays, 'had seen it nearly happen in Spain, and now it seemed inevitable. This time the gamble must come off, Revolution or Disaster. A series of defeats would topple the British ruling class; in the nick of time the People would kick them out and take control, snatching victory at the last moment.'

*Londoners eagerly read the latest war news, autumn 1939. Orwell considered it his duty to stay in London while the war was on.*

What Orwell wanted to happen did not happen. Britain did change between the years 1939 and 1945, culminating in the post-war election of a Labour government. There was also, during the war, a greater sense of social equality and the feeling that everyone should pull his or her weight. But there was no revolution nor any great desire to 'transform society from top to bottom' as Orwell proposed in *The Lion and the Unicorn* (1941), which contains the clearest expression of his views on the war, England and the sort of society he wished for. When the fighting was over, the general feeling was one of relief. After the war, Orwell wrote:

> Never would I have prophesied that we could go through nearly six years of war without arriving at either Socialism or Fascism. I don't know whether this semi-anaesthesia in which the British people contrive to live is a sign of decadence or a kind of instinctive wisdom.

He felt disillusioned:

> In the face of terrifying dangers and golden political opportunities, people just keep on in a sort of twilight sleep in which they are conscious of nothing except the daily round of work, family life, darts at the pub, exercising the dog, mowing the lawn, bringing home the supper beer.

In May 1940, as Hitler's army raced through the Low Countries and the collapse of France was imminent, the Orwells moved to a tiny, two-roomed flat in north London, to be nearer the hub of the home front. Orwell joined the Local Defence Volunteers, later re-named the Home Guard, and was made a sergeant. He took both his own duties and that of the Home Guard seriously. Describing it as a 'democratic guerilla force, like a more orderly version of the early Spanish Government militias', he thought that the Home Guard could become a sort of 'quasi-revolutionary People's Army', the vanguard of a people's revolution. His views were not shared by the government. Composed of men either too young or too old for military service, the Home Guard was formed to assist the regular forces in resisting a German invasion. In the event, its role was never tested, and with the German attack on the USSR in June 1941, fear of an invasion of England receded.

**Opposite** *Trooping down to an air-raid shelter on the day war was declared. The immediate destruction of London by aerial bombing that Orwell had predicted in* Coming Up For Air *failed to materialize. It was not until September 1940 that the first German bombers attacked London.*

Unable to take a more active part in the fighting, in August 1941 Orwell became a Talks Producer in the Empire Department of the BBC. 'Poetry on the air', he wrote, 'sounds like the Muses in striped trousers'. Although scrupulously fair in his reporting of the war, he nevertheless felt sullied by the propagandist role he had to play. His experiences at the BBC, it has been suggested, formed the basis for his portrayal of the Ministry of Truth in *Nineteen Eighty-Four*. After leaving the BBC, in November 1943 he took up the literary editorship of the left-wing weekly newspaper, *Tribune*. In a weekly column, 'As I Please', he was given the opportunity to write about almost any subject of interest to him – politics, books, love of fishing, walks in the country, cooking, gardening, and preserving the clarity of the English language. His style

**Opposite** *A member of the Home Guard handles a Lewis machine gun in his kitchen. After trying unsuccessfully to join the army, Orwell joined the Home Guard in 1940 and was made a sergeant.*

*Orwell broadcasts to India over the BBC Eastern Service. Orwell was a Talks Producer with the BBC from 1941 to 1943 and produced a monthly arts magazine called Voice.*

became even more relaxed, colloquial, direct and provocative – qualities which were to characterize his next major published work, *Animal Farm*.

In a preface written for the Ukrainian edition of the book (1947), Orwell explained its origins:

> . . . for the past ten years I have been convinced that the destruction of the Soviet myth was essential if we wanted a revival of the Socialist movement.
>
> On my return from Spain I thought of exposing the Soviet myth in a story that could be easily understood by almost anyone and which could be easily translated into other languages. However the actual details of the story did not come to me for some time until one day (I was then

**NATIONAL UNION OF JOURNALISTS**

7 John Street, Bedford Row, London, W.C.1

'Phone :
HOLborn 2258

Telegrams :
Natujay Holb, London

This is to certify that

Mr. GEORGE ORWELL

of The Tribune

is a member of the T.-+.P.
Branch of the National Union of Journalists.

Leslie R. Aldous Branch Sec.

(Address) 66. Priory Gans.. N.6.

Member's Sig.

*In November 1943 Orwell became Literary Editor of the left-wing socialist weekly newspaper Tribune. 'It was interesting', he later wrote, 'but it is not a period that I look back on with pride'.*

living in a small village) I saw a little boy, perhaps ten years old, driving a huge cart-horse along a narrow path, whipping it whenever it tried to turn. It struck me that if only such animals became aware of their strength we should have no power over them, and that men exploit animals in much the same way as the rich exploit the proletariat.

Orwell called his little book of some 30,000 words 'a fairy story'. The simplicity of the story and the language is, however, deceptive. Although read by children and used by those learning English as a model of good English prose, the style masks a profound political satire, in the same way as Swift's *Gulliver's Travels*, an attack on human folly, is widely regarded as a 'children's book'. *Animal Farm* is an allegory, chronicling the Russian Revolution from its inception in 1917 to Stalin's meeting with Churchill and Roosevelt at the Teheran Conference in 1943.

*Stalin, Roosevelt and Churchill at Teheran in 1943. Orwell satirized this meeting, between the leader of Soviet Russia and the leaders of capitalist Britain and the USA, in the final scene of* Animal Farm, *when Jones and his men dine with the pigs.*

*Napoleon followed by Snowball in a 1955 cartoon version of Animal Farm.*

The story opens with old Major, a 'Middle White boar', describing the appalling conditions under which the animals of Manor Farm are forced to live. In the same way that Karl Marx prophesied the overthrow of capitalism and the establishment of a worker's state in which all are free and equal, old Major envisages an animal rebellion against Man, and the establishment of a Utopian society in which the animals of England, free from human tyranny, live in harmony with one another, and all are well-fed and looked after. 'Man is the only real enemy we have', he says. 'Remove Man from the scene, and the root cause of hunger and overwork is abolished for ever . . . Only get rid of Man, and . . . almost overnight we could become rich and free'.

After the death of old Major, the pigs, 'the cleverest of the animals', begin preparing for the revolution. Two leaders emerge: Napoleon 'a large, rather fierce-looking Berkshire boar . . . with a reputation for getting his own way', and Snowball 'more vivacious . . . than Napoleon, quicker in speech and more inventive, but . . . considered not to have the same depth of character'. Napoleon is Stalin, Snowball is Trotsky, both leaders of the Russian Revolution. Jones the farmer, owner of Manor Farm, represents the Czarist regime, 'fallen on evil days'. The reversals and decadence of the ruling class in Russia during the First World War is represented by Jones having 'become much disheartened after losing money in a lawsuit', and his having 'taken to drinking more than was good for him'. After a heavy drinking spree Jones forgets to feed the animals. Driven by hunger, they take matters into their own hands and rebel. Jones is driven out and without fully understanding what has happened, the animals are left in charge.

Manor Farm is renamed Animal Farm and run on the principles of 'Animalism', the essential meaning of which is contained in seven simple 'commandments'. But almost

*Leon Trotsky, one of the leaders of the Russian revolution. Both Snowball in* Animal Farm *and Emmanuel Goldstein in* Nineteen Eighty-Four *were based on aspects of Trotsky's personality and career.*

immediately the seventh commandment, 'All animals are equal' is broken when the pigs requisition the milk for their sole use, which everyone assumes will be shared by all animals.

The events that follow closely mirror events in Russia. Jones, with the help of others, tries to retake Animal Farm in the same way that the Czarists tried to topple the Bolsheviks with the help of Britain and France. To face the threat of counter-revolution, the pigs consolidate their power. Personal rivalry between Napoleon and Snowball develops, culminating in the expulsion of Snowball from Animal Farm as Trotsky was exiled from the USSR in 1928. Left in sole charge, Napoleon establishes a military dictatorship. Snowball is declared a deadly enemy and blame for everything the animals suffer is laid at his feet. Seeing Snowball's agents everywhere, Napoleon murders innocent animals. Napoleon and his closest advisers take the best of the farm produce, enjoy privileges denied the other animals and rule by terror. For most of the animals life is no better than it had been under Jones. Gradually the principles of Animalism are utterly abandoned until a single commandment remains: 'ALL ANIMALS ARE EQUAL BUT SOME ANIMALS ARE MORE EQUAL THAN OTHERS.' Almost everything that old Major had believed in, that Snowball had fought for and the animals on the farm had suffered and worked hard for is not only abandoned but turned on its head. In the end the pigs are no longer distinguishable from Man.

*The behaviour of the pigs in* Animal Farm *was closely modelled on the Bolshevik bureaucracy in Soviet Russia. Like the Bolsheviks, the pigs control all aspects of life and take everything of the best for themselves.*

*Joseph Stalin, leader of Soviet Russia 1928–1953. Almost alone among left-wing intellectuals in the 1930s, Orwell saw that Stalin was a monstrous tyrant.*

Wittily told, full of humour and endearing characterization – such as the frivolous Mollie and cynical Benjamin – *Animal Farm* was the one book Orwell felt pleased with. He said of it: 'I tried, with full consciousness of what I was doing, to fuse political purpose and artistic purpose into one whole'. His success in achieving this, however, had unfortunate repercussions. Despite its simplicity, the meaning of *Animal Farm* is not obvious and has been misunderstood. To many conservatives in Britain and the USA the book shows how *all* revolutions, however idealistic in conception, inevitably lead to tyranny, a view Orwell did not share. Orwell's point was that Soviet Communism was a cynical betrayal of everything socialism meant.

Since its publication in 1945 *Animal Farm* remains the most effective *imaginative* exposure of what happened in Soviet Russia during the inter-war years, when some ten million people perished as a direct result of Stalin's policies. Even today the book is banned in the USSR. Predictably, its publication caused anger among communists all over the world, although this was nothing compared to the hysteria that was to greet *Nineteen Eighty-Four*, in 1949. To Orwell such a reaction was predictable. Did not Western communists continue to believe that Russia was a workers' paradise, despite all evidence to the contrary? Their refusal to see that Stalinism was a monstrous tyranny as bad as Nazi Germany, was, Orwell believed, a clear example of 'doublethink', the type of brainwashed beliefs described in *Nineteen Eighty-Four*.

Finishing the book in February 1944 Orwell had as much difficulty in getting it published as he had his early novels, despite his being an established author. Some publishers felt the time was not right for a book which attacked Soviet Russia, Britain's wartime ally. Not until the end of the war, in the summer of 1945, was the book to appear. Meanwhile, Orwell continued writing articles and reviews at an astonishing rate – 110 in 1944 alone. He was also thinking about and planning a new book, as he revealed in a letter to a friend in February 1944. After reading the dystopian novel *We* by the exiled Russian novelist Zamyatin, he wrote: 'I am interested in that kind of book and even keep making notes for one myself that may get written sooner or later'. *Nineteen Eighty-Four* was beginning to take shape.

*Orwell at work in his Islington flat, winter 1945. The success of* Animal Farm *made him one of the best-known writers in the English language.*

# 7 Towards *Nineteen Eighty-Four*

In March 1945, shortly before the end of the war in Europe, Orwell was in Germany reporting on conditions there for the London *Observer* when he received news that his wife had died. Seriously ill himself, he returned to England. On 17 August, three days after the Japanese surrender ended the Second World War, *Animal Farm* was published. The book soon became a best-seller. Fresh problems, both personal and public, beset him. His health was poor, he felt lonely after his wife's death and he now had a baby son, adopted in May 1944, to look after as well as a punishing work programme of articles and reviews to fulfil. The spectre of an atomic war troubled him deeply. The future, with the world divided into three 'super states' – one of the themes of *Nineteen Eighty-Four* – looked bleak.

In an article published in *Tribune* (1945), 'You and the Atom Bomb', he forecast something like the state of affairs that was to arise after the USSR exploded its own atomic bomb in 1949:

> Suppose – and really this is the likeliest development – that the surviving great nations make a tacit agreement never to use the atomic bomb against one another? Suppose they only use it, or the threat of it, against people who are unable to retaliate? In that case we are back where we were before, the only difference being that power is concentrated in still fewer hands and that the outlook for subject peoples and oppressed classes is still more hopeless . . .

Despite the defeat of fascism, the cause of political liberty had not been furthered. In England, Orwell warned in 'The Prevention of Literature' (1946), 'the immediate enemies of truthfulness, and hence the freedom of thought, are the press lords, the film magnates, and the bureaucrats'. Even writers and intellectuals, who should know better, were infected by totalitarian modes of thought, rarely speaking out in defence of liberty. In 'Politics and the English Language' (1946) he argued that 'the decline of language must ultimately have political and economic causes', and that 'orthodoxy, of whatever colour, seems to demand a lifeless, imitative style'. In *Nineteen Eighty-Four* 'orthodoxy means not thinking – not needing to think. Orthodoxy is unconsciousness'.

More was at stake than just 'good' writing. 'Political language . . . is designed to make lies sound truthful and murder respectable, and to give an appearance of solidity to pure wind.' Political language 'has to consist largely of euphemism, question-begging and sheer cloudy vagueness' because 'in our time, political speech and writing are largely the defence of the indefensible'. As an example he cites the word *pacification* – a word which was to be used by the Americans in Vietnam in the 1960s to describe their policies. What this seemingly innocuous word really describes, Orwell says, is a state of affairs in which 'defenceless villages are bombed from the air, the inhabitants driven out into the countryside, the cattle machine-gunned, the huts set on fire with incendiary bullets.'

*Orwell's work at the BBC, it has been claimed, provided the background for his description of the Ministry of Truth in* Nineteen Eighty-Four.

In the same year that Orwell wrote his three great essays on the relationship between language and politics – 'The Prevention of Literature', 'Politics and the English Language' and 'Politics vs Literature' – he began *Nineteen Eight-Four*. As in Stalin's USSR, language in Oceania has been so corrupted that words now mean their opposite. Outside the Ministry of Truth, where lies are concocted and propagated, Winston Smith reads 'the three slogans of the Party':

*The image of Big Brother dominates Victory Square where the inhabitants of London gather during Hate Week in a film version of Nineteen Eighty-Four.*

WAR IS PEACE
FREEDOM IS SLAVERY
IGNORANCE IS STRENGTH

When words cease to have any meaning, the loss of liberty is complete. 'Newspeak', the official language of Oceania, aims to remove all words which could lead people to think for themselves and question 'orthodoxy'. With a limited vocabulary, independent thought, the expression of personal wishes, desires, feelings and actions, is impossible. Control by the state, for the first time, is total. Once language is controlled, any thought or feeling other than that approved by the Party is literally unthinkable and unimaginable. In 1984 this has not yet happened. 'Oldspeak' words – i.e., words which existed before the Party took control – are still in use. The process of eliminating them is scheduled to be completed by the year 2050. Although words to formulate unorthodox thoughts still exist, such thoughts in 'Newspeak' are called 'thoughtcrime'.

Orwell described *Nineteen Eighty-Four* as 'a novel about the future – that is in a sense a fantasy, but in the form of a naturalistic novel'. From boyhood he had read and absorbed the works of the Utopian novelist, H.G.Wells. By the time he wrote *The Road to Wigan Pier*, however, Orwell rejected the vision of the future of Wells' early, optimistic works, as 'the paradise of little fat men'. Orwell's point was that even if such a world was realized – and in the essay 'Wells, Hitler and the World State' (1941) he argued that given the actual state of the world it was fantastic nonsense – it was also undesirable because it would be machine-governed and therefore less than human. More credible to Orwell's way of thinking were the dystopian novels *Under the Iron Heel* by Jack London (1902), Yevgeny Zamyatin's *We* (1924), Aldous Huxley's *Brave New World* (1932) and Wells' own more pessimistic novel *When the Sleeper Wakes* (1899).

*Rigid ranks of Italian Fascists with arms outstretched salute Benito Mussolini. The unthinking, regimented worship of Big Brother in* Nineteen Eighty-Four *was modelled on the leader worship common to all totalitarian regimes.*

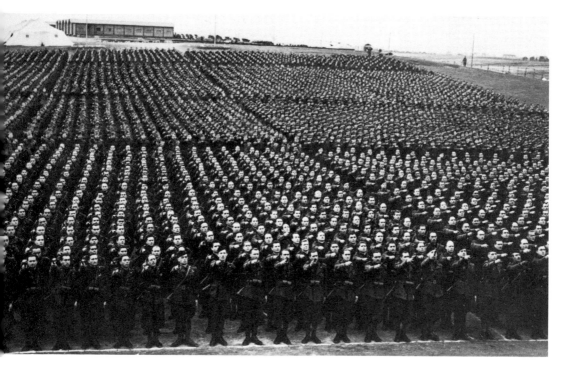

*Nineteen Eighty-Four*, however, differs from earlier dystopian novels in several important respects. In *Nineteen Eighty-Four* technology has not brought material comfort and leisure to the vast majority of people. In both *We* and *Brave New World* comfort has been achieved but only by sacrificing freedom. In *Nineteen Eighty-Four* there is neither. Food is inadequate, monotonous and synthetic, tobacco and chocolate are rationed and there is a shortage of the basic necessities of life such as razor blades – characteristics of London life during the Second World War and in the immediate post-war years. Technical innovation is directed solely at perfecting the instruments of war, state control and terror. By means of 'telescreens', two-way television, individuals are spied upon twenty-four hours a day. The Thought Police monitor thoughtcrime. Microphones are hidden even in the countryside.

The world in 1984 is divided into three power blocks, Oceania, Eurasia and Eastasia. Nominally in a state of semi-permanent war with one another, 'in one combination or another', in fact the three world empires prop one another up 'like three sheaves of corn'. England is Airstrip One, 'third most populous province of Oceania', and has as its capital London. The governing party of Oceania is Ingsoc (Newspeak for 'English Socialism'), and has been in power since the atomic war of the 1950s. Society is divided into three classes – the Inner Party, the Outer Party and the Proles. Their aims are 'entirely irreconcilable'. The Inner Party holds real power and is interested only in power, the Outer Party's function is to carry out the orders of the Inner Party, and the Proles, who form 85 per cent of the population, are discounted because they 'are not human beings'. Incapable of coherent thought, they live a sort of animal existence.

O'Brien, a member of the Inner Party, explains Ingsoc's philosophy of power:

> Power is inflicting pain and humiliation. Power is in tearing human minds to pieces and putting them together again in new shapes of your own choosing. Do you begin to see, then, what kind of world we are creating? It is the exact opposite of the stupid hedonistic Utopias that the old reformers imagined. A world of fear and treachery and torment, a world of trampling and being trampled upon, a world which will grow not less but more merciless as it refines itself. Progress in our world will be towards more pain.

'If you want a picture of the future of humanity', O'Brien says to Winston, 'imagine a boot stamping on a human face – for ever'. Truth is whatever the Party says it is. If the Party says that two plus two equals five, then it does. The Party's total control is summed up by the slogan, 'Who controls the past, controls the future: who controls the present controls the past'.

Winston Smith, prematurely aged at 39, is the last individualist, the last man to think and feel for himself. Watched all the time, he must never betray any emotion. 'Never show dismay! Never show resentment! A single flicker of the eyes could give you away.' He falls in love with Julia, a free-spirited, uninhibited girl of twenty-five

**Opposite** ' . . . the poster with the enormous face gazed from the wall. It was one of those pictures which are so contrived that the eyes follow you about when you move'.

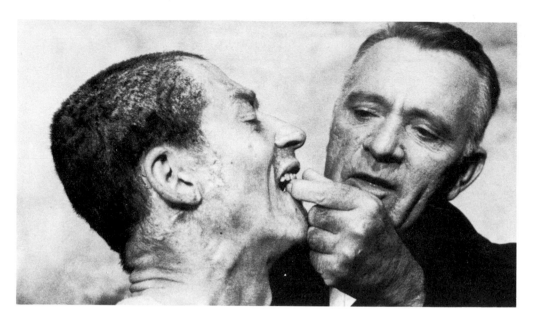

Winston Smith
suffers brutal
humiliation at the
hands of O'Brien.
John Hurt and
Richard Burton in
the 1984 film version
of Nineteen Eighty-
Four.

who appears to be a fanatical supporter of the Party but in reality is concerned only with enjoying herself. Her rebellion, says Winston, is purely 'from the waist down'. They meet whenever they can and make some sort of private life together in a bug-infested room above a junk shop in a district inhabited by proles. Both know and accept that sooner or later they will be caught:

'The one thing that matters', said Winston, 'is that we shouldn't betray one another, although even that can't make the slightest difference.'

'If you mean confessing,' she said, 'we shall do that, right enough. Everybody always confesses. You can't help it. They torture you.'

'I don't mean confessing. Confession is not betrayal. What you say or do doesn't matter: only feelings matter. If they could make me stop loving you – that would be the real betrayal.'

She thought it over. 'They can't do that,' she said finally. 'It's the one thing they can't do. They can make you say anything – *anything* – but they can't make you believe it. They can't get inside you.'

'No,' he said a little more hopefully, 'no; that's quite true. They can't get inside you. If you can *feel* that staying human is worthwhile, even when it can't have any result whatever, you've beaten them.'

**Opposite** *Julia in the 1955 film version of* Nineteen Eighty-Four. *Julia's attitude to life is that stated by Orwell in* The Road to Wigan Pier, *'It is almost impossible to be honest and to remain alive'.*

Staying human, then, is not betraying one another, not changing your love towards another human being. But this is just what 'they' succeed in making Winston and Julia do. In the end Winston and Julia feel nothing for each other. 'They' have 'got inside' them. When Winston is arrested and tortured his spirit is finally broken when confronted with the most terrible thing he can imagine – rats. In his agony he screams:

> Do it to Julia! Do it to Julia! Not me! Julia! I don't care what you do to her. Tear her face off, strip her to the bones. Not me! Julia! Not me!

His betrayal crushes him. He becomes just another faceless number. When he and Julia meet again they no longer have any feelings for one another. They agree that deep down 'all you care about is yourself'. The love they had once felt for each other is now directed towards Big Brother.

Why does Winston's and Julia's betrayal of each other have such a crushing effect? Many people, after all, would consider 'Do it to Julia!' and 'all you care about is yourself' to be simply 'human nature'. The reason why Orwell thought this to be the most terrible thing a human being could say is stated in 'Reflections on Gandhi', an essay written in 1949 after completing *Nineteen Eighty-Four*:

> The essence of being human is . . . that one is prepared in the end to be defeated and broken by life, which is the inevitable price of fastening one's love upon other human individuals.

If you are not prepared to sacrifice yourself for those you love, you are worthless. Finally, it is the only weapon the individual has of preserving his or her integrity. Gordon Comstock in *Keep the Aspidistra Flying* was in a sense 'defeated and broken by life' by 'fastening' his love upon Rosemary. In *Nineteen Eighty-Four* this is no longer possible. Winston is unable to pay the price and consequently becomes less than human.

*A meeting of the Anti-Sex League in* Nineteen Eighty-Four. *In Oceania the suppression of sex is essential for the survival of the Party. 'Sexual privation induced hysteria, which was desirable because it could be transformed into war-fever and leader-worship'.*

Some hope of a better future, or at least a future in which humanity is not entirely crushed, *is* present in the book. 'If there is hope', writes Winston in his dairy, 'it lies in the proles' – Orwell's attitude in *The Road to Wigan Pier*. But, as Winston recognizes, this poses a dilemma, for 'until they [the proles] become conscious they will never rebel, and until after they have rebelled they cannot become conscious'. And Winston sees nothing to suggest that they will rebel.

Orwell completed the first draft of *Nineteen Eighty-Four* in October 1947 at Barnhill, the farmhouse on the island of Jura (population 250), off the Scottish coast in which he had lived since December 1946. 'I have been in lousy health most of this year', he wrote a friend after finishing the novel, 'my chest as usual'. On Christmas Eve 1947 he entered Hairmyres Hospital, near Glasgow. He was to remain there for seven months. The chest trouble which had plagued him all his life was now diagnosed as tuberculosis, for which, at the time, there was no cure. In July 1948 he returned to Jura, completing the final draft of *Nineteen Eighty-Four* in November. He began planning future essays, stories and novels and wrote the occasional review and article, but in January 1949, his health broken, he was admitted to a sanatorium at Cranham in Gloucestershire.

*The isolated farmhouse of Barnhill on the Scottish island of Jura where Orwell wrote* Nineteen Eighty-Four.

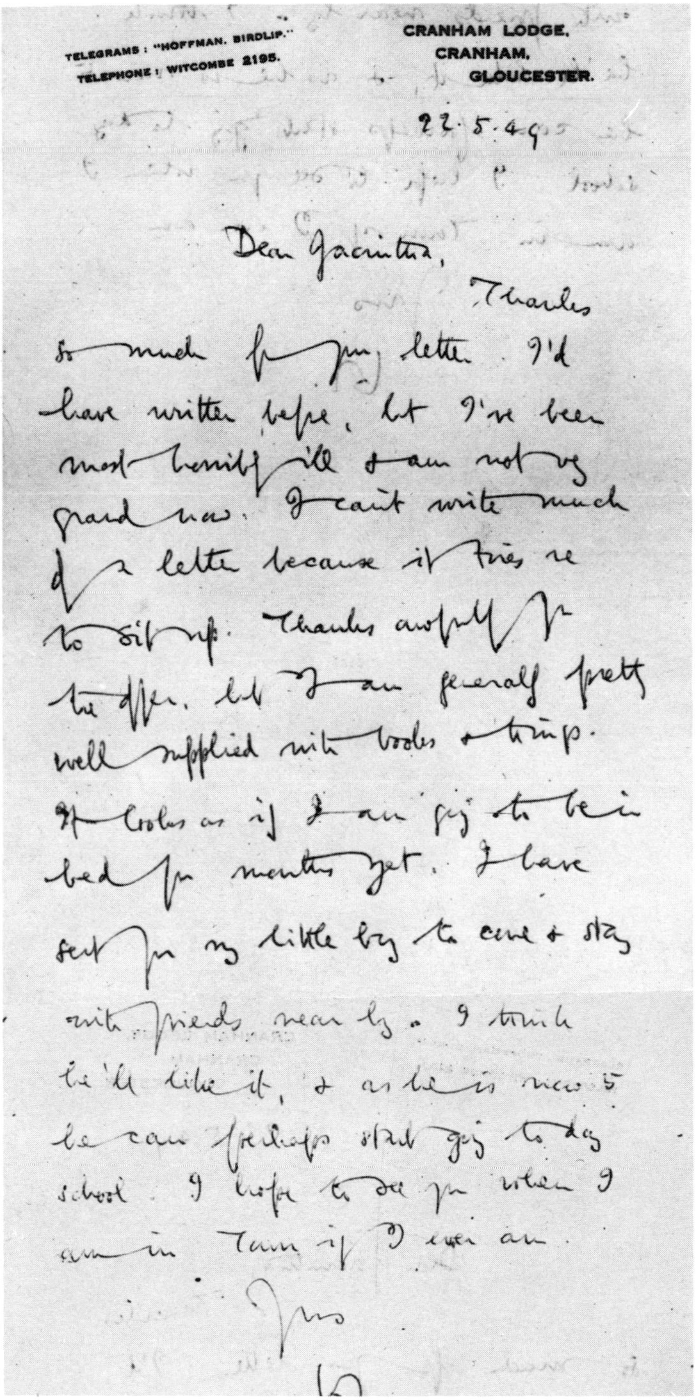

CRANHAM LODGE.
CRANHAM.
GLOUCESTER.

TELEGRAMS: "HOFFMAN. BIRDLIP."
TELEPHONE: WITCOMBE 2195.

22.5.49

Dear Jacintha,

Thanks so much for your letter. I'd have written before, but I've been most horribly ill & am not very grand now. I can't write much of a letter because it tires me to sit up. Thanks awfully for the offer, but I am generally pretty well supplied with books & things. It looks as if I am going to be in bed for months yet. I have sent you my little boy to care & stay with friends near by. I think he'll like it, & as he is now 5 he can perhaps start going to day school. I hope to see you when I am in Town if I ever am.

Yrs
Geo

*One of the last letters Orwell wrote from Cranham sanatorium to his childhood friend Jacintha Buddicom.*

*Nineteen Eighty-Four* was published in June 1949 and became an instant best-seller. In the USA it was selected as 'The Book of the Month'. Dismayed by the way in which the book was interpreted by some reviewers, Orwell dictated a statement from his bed refuting the claim that it was a prophesy of what would happen 'inside the next forty years'. 'This is not correct', he said, 'I think that, allowing for the book being after all a parody, something like *Nineteen Eighty-Four* could happen . . . The moral to be drawn from this dangerous nightmare situation is a simple one: *Don't let it happen. It depends on you.*'

Soon after publication of the book, Orwell was moved to University College Hospital, London. There, on 13 October 1949, he married Sonia Brownell, whom he had known since 1945. Plans were made for him to go to a private sanatorium in Switzerland. A set of fishing rods was placed at the foot of his bed in anticipation. On 21 January 1950, on the night before his departure, George Orwell had a haemorrhage and died alone. He was 46 years of age.

*Sonia Brownell in
October 1949. Orwell
wrote of his marriage
to Sonia Brownell:
'everyone will be
horrified . . . I really
think I should stay
alive longer if I were
married'.*

# Glossary

**Allegory**  The treatment of a subject under the guise of a story in which the meaning is conveyed by a series of symbols.

**Anarchism**  Literally 'absence of law and government'. In fact, political anarchists such as those Orwell encountered in Spain believe in a society of self-governing communes, each working for the common good, based on trade unions, professions and other societies.

**Authoritarian**  A dictatorial form of government under which there is little personal freedom.

**Churchill,**  Winston Spencer (1874–1965). British Prime Minister 1940–45.

**Colloquial**  A style of writing approximating common speech or conversation.

**Communism**  A theory of society advocated by Karl Marx in which all private property is abolished. A term applied, mistakenly in Orwell's belief, to describe the system of government in the USSR.

**Czarist**  The system of government which existed in Russia before the revolution of 1917. Derived from Czar – the emperor of Russia.

**Democracy**  A form of society in which the authority of the government is vested in all the people.

**Doublethink**  A Newspeak word meaning the ability to hold two contradictory beliefs at the same time.

**Dystopian**  Imagined place, state or situation in which conditions and the quality of life are dreadful. The opposite of Utopian.

**Fascism**  A system of harsh authoritarian rule first established in Italy in 1923.

**Feudal**  The social system prevalent in Western Europe between the ninth and sixteenth centuries, in which landowners exerted great power, granting their tenants land in return for their loyalty, hard work and military service.

**Hitler**, Adolf (1886-1945). Leader of the Nazi Party and dictator of Germany 1933–1945.

**I.L.P.** Independent Labour Party, a British left-wing socialist, anti-communist political party. Orwell was a member from 1938–39.

**Imperialism** The establishment of an empire and the, often tyrannical, subjugation of one people by another.

**Marx**, Karl (1818-83). German founder of modern communism.

**Nazism** The theory and practice of the German Nazi (National Socialist) Party.

**Polemic** Taking a particular side in an argument or controversy.

**P.O.U.M.** Partido Obrero de Unificacion Marxista (Workers United Marxist Party). A Spanish revolutionary socialist, anti-communist party 1935–37.

**Propaganda** The broadcast, transmission or spreading of opinions and principles. Often used to mean the spreading of biased or even false information.

**Roosevelt**, Franklin Delano (1882–1945). President of the USA 1932–1945.

**Stalin**, Joseph (1879–1953). Russian Communist and dictator of the USSR 1928–1953.

**Soviet myth** Orwell's term for the mistaken belief held by Western intellectuals and workers that the USSR was truly a socialist state.

**Totalitarian** A form of government exercising complete control over every facet of society and permitting no opposition.

**Trotsky**, Leon (1879-1940). One of the leaders of the Russian Revolution, exiled by Stalin in 1928 and murdered by his agents in 1940.

**Utopia** Literally 'nowhere', from the Greek. Commonly used to describe an ideal society of the future. Writers have often used such a vision of the future to discuss or satirize traits already present in society.

# List of dates

**Life**

| | |
|---|---|
| **1903** | 25 June: born Eric Arthur Blair at Motihari, Bengal, India. |
| **1904** | Comes to England with his mother and lives in Henley-on-Thames, Oxfordshire. |
| **1911** | Attends St. Cyprian's School, Eastbourne, Sussex. |
| **1917** | At the top public school, Eton, as a King's Scholar. |
| **1921** | Christmas: leaves Eton. |
| **1922** | November: arrives in Mandalay, Burma, as probationary Assistant Superintendent of Police in the Indian Imperial Police Force. |
| **1928** | January: resigns from the Indian Police. Lives in London and makes expeditions to the East End to learn about low life. Goes to Paris to write. |
| **1929** | February: in the Hôpital Cochin in Paris with pneumonia. Autumn: working as a 'plongeur', (dish-washer) in a Paris hotel. Returns to England before Christmas. |
| **1930** | Tramping and hop-picking in Kent. From his parents' home in Southwold, Suffolk, makes excursions to London and the Home Counties (the counties bordering London) as a tramp. |
| **1932** | Teaching at The Hawthornes, a private school at Hayes, Middlesex. |

| 1933 | Abandons teaching after another attack of pneumonia. Living with his parents at Southwold. Adopts pseudonym 'George Orwell'. |
|------|--------------------------------------------------------------------------------------------------------------------------|
| 1934 | October: moves to London, working part-time as an assistant in a Hampstead bookshop. |
| 1936 | Travels to the north of England to report on the conditions of the working class. Moves to Wallington, Hertfordshire. Marries Eileen O'Shaughnessy. Outbreak of the Spanish Civil War. Goes to Spain and joins the P.O.U.M. militia, on the Republican side. |
| 1937 | Witnesses the Stalinist purge of P.O.U.M. in Barcelona. 10 May wounded in the throat. Escapes to France in June. |
| 1938 | March: ill with tuberculosis. Goes to Morocco to convalesce. |
| 1939 | Returns to England in March. 3 September: Britain at war with Germany. |
| 1940 | Moves to London. Joins the Home Guard. |
| 1941 | Talks Producer with the BBC. |
| 1943 | Resigns from the BBC. Becomes literary editor of *Tribune*. Writes *Animal Farm*. |
| 1944 | Adopts baby son, Richard Horatio Blair. |
| 1945 | Wife dies. End of the Second World War. |
| 1947 | Living at Barnhill, Jura, Scotland. |
| 1948 | Deteriorating health. Enters Hairmyres Hospital, Glasgow. Finishes *Nineteen Eighty-Four*. |
| 1949 | At Cranham Sanatorium, Gloucestershire. Transfers to |

| | University College Hospital, London. Seriously ill. Marries Sonia Brownell. |
|---|---|
| **1950** | 21 January: George Orwell dies. |

**Works**

| | |
|---|---|
| **1933** | *Down and Out in Paris and London* |
| **1934** | *Burmese Days* |
| **1935** | *A Clergyman's Daughter* |
| **1936** | *Keep the Aspidistra Flying* |
| **1937** | *The Road to Wigan Pier* |
| **1938** | *Homage to Catalonia* |
| **1939** | *Coming Up For Air* |
| **1940** | *Inside the Whale* |
| **1941** | *The Lion and the Unicorn* |
| **1945** | *Animal Farm* |
| **1946** | *Critical Essays* |
| **1947** | *The English People* |
| **1949** | *Nineteen Eighty-Four* |
| **1950** | *Shooting An Elephant* |
| **1953** | *England Your England* |

# Further reading

**Biography**

CRICK, B. *George Orwell: A Life* (Secker & Warburg, 1981, Penguin, 1987)

FYVEL, T.R. *George Orwell: A Personal Memoir* (Macmillan, 1982)

GROSS, M. *The World of George Orwell* (Weidenfeld & Nicolson, 1972)

STANSKY, P. and ABRAHAMS, W. *The Unknown Orwell* (Constable, 1972); *Orwell: The Transformation* (Constable, 1979)

WADHAMS, S. *Remembering George Orwell* (Penguin, 1984)

**Critical works**

MEYERS, J. *A Reader's Guide to George Orwell* (Thames & Hudson, 1975)

REES, R. *George Orwell: Fugitive from the Camp of Victory* (Secker & Warburg, 1961)

SMITH, D. and MOSHER, M. *Orwell For Beginners* (Writers and Readers, 1984)

WILLIAMS, R. *George Orwell* (Fontana, 1971)

WOODCOCK, G. *The Crystal Spirit: A Study of George Orwell* (Penguin, 1970)

WYKES, D. *A Preface to George Orwell* (Longman, 1987)

**Editions**

All Orwell's novels and essays are available in paperback published by Penguin together with *The Collected Essays, Journalism and Letters* in four volumes, edited by Sonia Orwell and Ian Angus. A new *Collected Works of George Orwell* has recently been published by Secker & Warburg, edited by Peter Davison, and includes material not previously published or reprinted.

The scripts Orwell wrote while working at the BBC 1941–43, have been published under the title *The War Broadcasts* (Duckworth/BBC, 1985)

**Background reading**

DEUTSCHER, I. *Stalin* (Penguin, 1976)
KOESTLER, A. *Darkness at Noon* (Penguin, 1984)
LONDON, J. *The People of the Abyss; Under the Iron Heel*
MITCHELL, D. *The Spanish Civil War* (Granada 1982)
MUGGERIDGE, M. *The Thirties: 1930 – 1940 in Great Britain* (Collins, 1967)
WILSON, B. *To the Finland Station* (Fontana 1969)
ZAMYATIN, Y. *We* (Penguin, 1987)

# Index

# Picture acknowledgments

The author and publishers would like to thank the following for allowing their illustrations to be reproduced in this book: Aldus Archive 47; BBC Hulton Picture Library 14-15, 20-21, 31, 36, 38 39, 40, 54, 55, 57, 60, 74; Billie Love Historical Collection 11, 32, 78; E.T. Archive 44, 86; Nigel Flynn 58, 59, 70, 75, 90; Mary Evans Picture Library 61, 66; National Film Archive 82, 84, 89, 94; Popperfoto 48, 49, 56, 62, 72, 73, 81, 83; Princeton University Library 43; Topham Picture Library 41, 46, 63, 71, 76, 91, 92, 95, 96, 97; University College London 7, 8, 9, 10, 13, 16, 18, 22, 24, 25, 27, 28, 29, 33, 35, 50, 51, 52, 64, 65, 67, 68, 79, 80, 88, 98, 99, 100, 101; Wayland 85.